The Reunion Float

The Reunion Float

Poems by

Kevin Shyne

Cover art by Mary C. Shyne, daughter of the author,
inspired by a Beth McDonald photo on Unsplash

ISBN: 978-1-63980-626-3

Kelsay Books
502 South 1040 East, A-119
American Fork, Utah 84003
Kelsaybooks.com

For Debi Shyne, love of my life,
for my beautiful daughters, Laura and Mary
for my remarkable brothers and sisters—
Stephen, Joanna, William, Susan, Christopher and Laura—
for Nancy Friedlander, extraordinary teacher and encourager
&
in memory of James and Eleanor Shyne

Acknowledgments

Thank you to the following publications, in which versions of these poems previously appeared:

Poetry Breakfast: "Judy and Clark," "Sleepless on a Train"
Poetry Porch: "But No One Comes," "Second Father"
The Road Not Taken: "The Book Return"

Contents

Four *Why Disregard Your Human Splendor?*

Five *The Reunion Float*

One

Set the Delicates on Gentle Rinse

All the Difference

It’s one thing to write
when you’re alone
when you’re aware
that no one else is there,
but it’s something else again
to know that someone cares
about the writer in the room upstairs.

Even though the tapping of the keyboard,
the bird calls, the traffic noise outside,
the ticking of the clock and dripping
of the faucet are the same,
the silence differs,
as if it had a more familiar name.

I could crack the door and listen
or lay a hand upon the needlecraft you paused,
too tired to lay another stitch
or start the wash both of us forgot to run
much less to set the delicates on gentle rinse.

But there’s no need.
The comfort of your presence
makes all the difference.

A Place to Call Your Own

Once you've made a house a home
prepare to shiver
when the freezer ices over.
When gutters clog with leaves
the overflow runs down your neck.
When the toilet seat
comes off its hinges,
you feel unhinged
beset by brokenness.
Or when the sink coughs up its dreck
you are the soggy mess.

To you, apartment dwellers,
envious of friends not paying rent,
to own seems simple,
more secure and permanent,
but best beware
a house will take you in,
hook you on the sheen
of hardwood floors
refinished on your knees.
You've been warned
about upgrading trim and countertop.
Even though you've sworn
no more, you've gone too far to stop.

First-time buyers,
try to understand
when you think you've bagged a plum
you're wrong. The house has had it planned
all along. It whispers *Come!*

You’ve been singled out to turn the key
that makes a house a home.
The ending’s meant to be
a place to call your own.

My Perfect Hostess

When visitors arrive, you attend to every need
except your own, unmet,
deprived of opportunity.
Before too long you'll be
as affection starved
as the Tin Man known as me.

Over time we've learned
to give and take embraces
only we can see, a touch,
a brush of fingers.
Mine are made of metal,
yours of Dorothy.

Guests needn't know
what's going on or how we'll compensate
for love deferred or how we'll carry on
when the company,
the last of them, at last,
is out the door and gone.

The Kettle

The whistle's rising pitch
brought me back to when
there were no microwaves,
to when you'd set a kettle on the stove.

Years later in the cottage,
that became a second home,
I could have zapped
the water in my cup.

Instead, I filled a kettle,
turned the burner dial
to Hi and went back to my book,
waiting for the boiling water's note
the steaming tea to brew.

Some days a microwave
will never do.

Second Father

Why did I wait so long to write to you,
more than a friend, a second father,
until your Christmas letters stopped?
In free and easy cursive, you'd tell
the news of Hannah, adopted daughter,
Pat, the wife you married late in life,
your children by an ex with children of their own.
If only I'd written sooner instead of writing a poem.

Why did I wait so long to call
until your story-telling voice and poetry
you knew by heart no longer could
uplift me through the phone?
No church confessor listened half as well
or knew the words to say
to guide a young man home.
If only I'd called you sooner instead of writing a poem.

Why did I wait so long to catch a flight
until no wings could take me where
you hugged me at your open door?
As close as strings of a mandolin,
as rows of wheat, as drops of rain,
we could have mused for hours about
how beautiful and foolish this old world had grown.
If only I'd caught a flight instead of writing a poem.

How could I let it come to this—the father
whom I idolized was gone before our work was done.
Then came an unexpected gift,
the second father you'd become.

I'd gladly be the man forever in your debt,
leaning on your strength, blessing you, and yet,
so much we left unfinished. Shouldn't I have known?
If only I'd told you sooner instead of writing a poem.

Holy Innocents

Our dear mother, high school valedictorian,
stepped off the fast-track
only to discover,
there are naturals in every sport and art,
even mothering, and she,
to her chagrin, she wasn't one.
Learning on the job
with a first and second son,
a daughter on the way
but no one there to share the load.
Our patient father, engineer, New Englander,
but not an empathetic listener,
packed up our sunny California life
for a more familiar coast
in hopes proximity to grandparents
would ease a stressed-out wife.

Instead the load increased.
Pestered by her husband's mother,
her own parents too frail and cranky to be
of much assistance,
in consultation with the parish priest
she agreed to temporary placement
in an orphanage
for a docile younger son,
until they'd found a rental
far enough away to keep
the relatives from dropping by.

Our poor mother, at wit's end,
remembered when success had come so easily
in high school, college, her career,

but with a family of seven
always on the run
it took years for her to see
how splendidly she'd done.

As for me, I had two months of being
coddled by the Sisters of Holy Innocents.
In spite of all you hear about abusive orphan keepers,
the good nuns loved their one-year-old,
a beam of sunshine in a gray New England spring.

They left an imprint on my infant brain,
not erased but overprinted,
the underlying goodness left intact.

I write this poem now in thanks to Holy Innocents,
to Sisters who as if on cue
became like angels to the Shynes
coming to our mother's rescue,
not to mention mine.

Lost Glove

I found my water bottle cap
in the strainer of the kitchen sink,
a cherished souvenir
of a hiking victory.

Encouraged by my daughters
I stopped to drink
electrolyte solutions,
baby-stepped the switchbacks,
caught my breath,
hauled my bony body up
on hand- and footholds
made from massive chains
embedded in the unforgiving rock
until we stood on Angels Landing
in Zion National Park,
two daughters into women grown
while I, as if in time reversed,
embraced a younger comfort zone.

Years later, the present would intrude
on Zion memory.
I rinsed the bottle, took a drink
the cap discovered
in the sudsy kitchen sink
whose finding coincided
with the loss of gloves
well worn by cycling.

Two weeks went by before
I found the right-hand glove
on a trailside bench.

I’d either left it accidentally
or some unknown rider
retrieved and set it down
where a passerby might see.

I slipped it on, the leather stiff
from time out in the weather.
I searched but could not find its mate
one ride, two gloves, two different fates.

In time I came to realize,
the bottle cap in one hand,
the glove in the other,
these souvenirs would symbolize
my dearest gains and losses.
Some are found
for reasons never understood
while others, loved as much
if lost are gone for good.

The Grown-Up Table

Last Thanksgiving
when the silver and good china
made their semi-annual appearance,
when dinner ended in contented sighs,
when elders pushed back their plates,
when children occupied themselves
with board games and comic books
cluttering a folding table,
we invited grandson Logan, age 11, to sit with us.

Since last year's holiday
he's stronger, taller, more aware,
a confident observer
absorbing words and meanings
to be reflected on
in the quiet of his room.

While grown-ups cleared the table,
poured coffee and shuffled cards,
Logan reunited with his younger kin
pleased by his return
to the role of go-between
from child to grown-up company.

The years will lift him up
draw him in and set aside
the sensibility that growing up disables
making him a stranger
to parts he can no longer play.
The present slides away.
The future turns the tables.

Two

So Much We'll Never Know

But No One Comes

Stop America!
Do not avert your eyes
from children at Uvalde
sons and daughters seized
as if by Abraham, his hand raised
except today no angel's hand
was poised to stay the blade.

America, don't look away.
Don't mute the sound.
Don't dim the lights.

When the gunman entered
When he fired his guns
When teachers shielded innocents
When children grasped their phones
When victim after victim fell
When families identified the dead by bloodied clothing
When the living saw the splatter on classroom walls.

Where were the lights, the lost lights of the children?
Did they ripple, swirl in eddies or disappear around a bend?

How could the day have come to such an end?

America, remember goodness gone.
Listen to their song.
A child dials 911
whispers *Please send police*
but no one comes.

So Much We'll Never Know

His finger pulled the trigger.
That we know
but what hand pushed
aside a helping hand?
What mind devised
a one-way plan
to make him think
he wasn't seen and didn't matter?

Was the last thing he said
I'm already dead
and the act, the shot,
only confirmed the fact?

Cold Comfort

The world doesn't know how close
I am to bingeing all night.
The click of the key
as I lock my door
will comfort me more
than the world ever did for me.

When I was young
the world didn't care
if anyone (everyone!) teased
me about my weight.
I never asked for a size and shape
that nobody wanted to be.

The world taught me to say
that names can never hurt me
but how I wish the same ordeal—
chubby, tubby, fatso, cow—
upon the world for just one day
then tell me how unhurt it feels.

It was more of the same,
no worse, at home
portion-controlled (groan!)
by faces of stone.
God forbid if I asked for more.
How I longed to be left alone.

Fast forward to my life today.
After putting me down for 20-plus years,
the world says, *Spread your wings and soar!*
Be your own best friend.
You're beautiful, inside and out.
My God, I can't take any more!

Here's what the world needs to know of comfort—
imagine you're on a starvation diet
on the run from a third world war.
What would you give for a moment of quiet
in front of an open freezer door,
or walking away, brown bag in hand
from a 24-hour convenience store?

Baby Blue

Our third grandchild died unborn,
an embryonic boy or girl
who might have gone to God
unnamed and uncompleted as our grief
had not our grandson spoken up.

Ten weeks along, our daughter Laura
saw blots of blood on toilet tissue.
By noon, the bleeding stained a towel.
The midwife called her back and said
Get off the phone and go.

Entering the hospital alone, she took each step
as if the slightest bump would open up a wound.
After husband Jeremy arrived, under artificial light
in semi-privacy afforded by a flimsy drape,
they heard the doctor say their child was gone.
His sympathetic explanation came to this:
a tiny heart has stopped, we don't know why.

Two months before a humble urine drop
had heralded the news
as if a testing kit could blare
like trumpets from a mountaintop.
Soon enough they told their toddler sons,
careful not to cause the boys to feel displaced
but elevated by big brotherhood.
Then came the day I couldn't help myself.
Have you chosen names? I asked. *Too soon,*
they said. I took the secret in their smile
to mean too soon to say.

The ringing of a telephone would end my wait.
Reading in our living room, my wife and I
could not have guessed how close we were to grief.
She set aside her book, reached for the phone,
and hearing Laura's voice, mouthed her name to me.
I shivered when her hand went to her mouth.
With broken voice she said, *We're on our way.*

Laura met us at the door, Jeremy beside her,
faces strained by keeping grief in check,
not wanting to upset their sons,
Clark plotting mayhem quietly,
Logan rushing forward with a thousand things to say.
Throughout our stay, the sounds of their rambunctious
play could not displace the silence of prenatal
medicines removed from pantry shelves,
of newborn outfits folded into storage boxes,
of monthly midwife visits crossed off calendars,
of trudging past our disappointed joy.

I did my part, playing with the boys, helping where I could,
while stumbling through an inner haze, as if wounded
on a battlefield, too numb or too afraid to look
to see how badly I was hurt.
In such misery, what good is God or prayer?
You ask too much, my Son, who are so richly blessed,
He seemed to say, and yet I could not help but ask,
What would it hurt to give the child another day?
Each night we wrestled, God and I. When I awoke defeated,
the echo of His question silenced my reply,
Would there ever be a day it hurt you less to say goodbye?

A gray week passed before a word was spoken to the boys.
On Laura's lap at bedtime, Jeremy straddling
the recliner's arm, Clark and Logan
turned familiar pages. When the story ended
Laura paused, closed the book and said,
The baby we were waiting for has gone to heaven.
Clark pressed his crew-cut head to Laura's side
while Logan pondered what he'd heard.
In days to come, Laura would recall their hush
as if they listened for an infant sleeping near.

In a night light's glow, she and Jeremy
tucked in and kissed the boys.
Retreating to the hall they heard, astonished,
Logan raise his head and whisper,
Good night, Baby Blue.

When Laura called next day
to tell of Logan's christening,
I sprouted wings and flew. In a flash
I understood everything had changed.
The child we thought we'd never know
had come home with a name
as if to mark a spirit's course
briefly passing through
that we might bless the child we mourned
Good night Baby Blue.

Two in a Bush

A thicket stirred drew in my eye—
a bird, feathers fluffed amid
last season's growth of branch and sprig,
disclosed by a shadow's shake.

I am such a bird,
my mind stripped bare of foliage
sheltering within a cloud of twigs
secured by little more than faith.

What sort of refuge do we share?
the bird half frozen, half asleep,
seems to answer with a question,
a test of my belief—

Which of us will be the first
to quit our poor retreat?

Titanic Me

Today I fixed a storm door lock
diverted a flooding gutter
submitted a poem to a magazine
grilled a steak to perfection
caught up with siblings on a video chat
called my high school English teacher,
long retired, and made her laugh.
So why at the end of a most
commendable, blue-ribbon day
am I on emotional tiptoes,
writing my way as well as I can
out of an Irish funk
keeping my nose above the swell
on a ship that supposedly couldn’t be sunk?

Three

Learner's Permit

Forest Parquetry

In an autumn wood
a maple leaf descends
more slowly than it should
as if to make amends
to limbs it leaves behind.
It spirals in the air before
the forest carpenters design
a golden tiled floor.

The Book Return

I have no wish to skydive when I'm old
nor bicycle from Istanbul to Rome
nor sled behind a husky team
from Anchorage to Nome.
But Lord, grant me mobility
for excursions to the library
with books recirculated
to patrons after me.

Or, if pressed for time
I'll turn into the drive-through lane
to drop bar-coded books
into the outdoor slot.
Unerringly discerned
by a scanner's flash,
each book is welcomed back
with a cordial slap
from the rain-proof flap
of the all-night book return.

Sleepless on a Train

The puppy sun
licks at my face
not letting me sleep.

I wake aboard
an inbound train
uncurling in my seat.

A man flips through
a file, his office formed
by knees and shirt.

His neighbor's paper
crinkles, each page crying
Read me first!

Pre-teens pose
in *Hello Kitty* clothes
as if in a mirror.

Twin earbud boys
sway with wires
dangling from their ears.

A romance novel
smolders where
a lady marks her page.

The train conductor
twirls his punch,
the sheriff on an Old West stage.

Early bird commuters
ride on tracks
within their minds.

Their dreams derail
at 6:03, awake
at the end of the line.

Learner's Permit

Although a book can't love you back
it can slide over from the driver's seat
roll down the window and say,
Hop in.

The Sprinkler

In the blazing August sun
my lawn is an old pair of khakis
worn thin, stitched and patched
a flimsy memory of a favorite pair
cut off at the knees.
Jealous of the lawn next door
luxuriantly green, while mine
is parched, a wardrobe of hay
without a belt to hold it up
slipping off my hips
taunted by a sprinkler singing
shick, shick, shick, shick, shick.
Swept by the spray
the neighbor's turf
may condescend to glisten,
or gossip with its withered peers
if any care to listen.

The Novice

Our daughter, second grader,
addresses valentines,
adorning them with stickers,
mastering the lessons of affection
masquerading as a game.
Some cards she signs with question marks.
Others she initials.
On a few she spells her name.

Never Lose Your Keys Again

Make a list of often misplaced stuff,
your phone, the keys, your pen and such.
Chose a place for each,
as obvious as the ceramic bowl
on the kitchen counter.
Try to understand—
no other holding place allowed
except your hand.

Take a moment with each item.
Feel its shape and texture. Make a promise to yourself,
regardless of the hurry, inconvenience or distraction,
you'll set it in its designated place.

Now comes the hard part—
You're heading out the door,
the phone rings and a neighbor
says this won't take long.

You try to seem engrossed,
no finger-tapping,
no emptying the dryer
no smoothing out the
wrinkles in your jeans.

Half an hour later,
free to run your errands,
you realize the keys are gone.
The phone is nowhere to be seen.

You rummage through the catch-all drawer
turn your pockets inside out
circle back to places checked
three times before.
You shake your head
confounded. It's the same old show.
The cast of misplaced things
seems to have a hiding place
somewhere you cannot go.

The ceramic bowl
rolls its eyes
as always in the know
whispering familiar words
Old friend, I told you so!

Reading in Bed

A book is a house in the woods.
The cover is the welcome mat.
The pages are the rooms.
The margins are the trim.
The sentences are windows
to let the daylight in.
The numbers on the pages
tell you where you've been
The print implores you to explore
this roomy inner space.

The Workout

A poet's fitness
comes not from calisthenics
lifting weights or miles of distance run
but from making room in bed
for a word or phrase to come.

Aroused at such an hour,
the poet grumbles.
Bare feet on cold floor,
not quite awake but on the brink,
he fumbles for a pen and paper scrap
to catch a metaphor
in a trap of ballpoint ink.

Back in bed, he thinks,
It looks so simple
as if poems were written on demand
or lines would come to mind upon command.
Subconsciously he knows
why nothing else compares
to the way a poem grows
or how a poet lives by breathing underwater
as if the dreams were air.

Drowsing off to sleep,
the turn of phrase secured,
the poet rocks in time
his mind a playground swing.
It's good, the dreamer sighs,
It seems to sing.

Four

Why Disregard Your Human Splendor?

Purgatory Gets a Bad Name

In light of my life story
my afterlife will pass
through purgatory.
Not that I'll mind
a waiting room
the Lord designed
to mend our moral mettle
or any other business
left unsettled.

For wouldn't a God
who sees our fears
be pleased by the sight
of brothers and sisters finally
getting it right
after getting it wrong for years?

Next door to heaven
what other place soothes the needs
of those who crave amends
caught in the act of wrapping up
a few loose ends?

Some souls will try
to hustle by, but why not
make the most of purgatory
where sins are real
but not the end of the story?

The last words
on the last page
of the scripture set within you
are not, like death, *The End*
but like grace, *To Be Continued.*

Easter Morning

Hope shines in the East
abundant but a distant feast
while Faith proceeds where it is led
thankful for its daily bread.

Love brings in the harvest
heavy on the vine
a wedding gift from One who turns
water into wine.

At break of day, the world beholds
a masterpiece of grace
painted by the hand of hope
hanging on a nail of faith.

God Knows

Your picture
is on God’s bedroom dresser
in the photo sleeve of His wallet
on His most-wanted poster
your face above the caption
My Beloved One

Why disregard
your human splendor?
You turn from God and yet
He remembers
your likeness to a newborn Son.

More Blessed to Give

Shine for the weary
unaware of being held dear.

Shine for people too distraught
to know the joy their presence brought.

Shine for teachers full of grief
for students too far gone to reach.

Shine for healers' misery
beneath the cross of empathy.

Shine for scholars unafraid of burning
at the stake of fear of learning.

Shine for all who bear the mark
of years in God's employ.

Shine that they may know the arc
of suffering bends toward joy.

The Girl in the Picture

Napalm is very powerful but faith, forgiveness and love are much more powerful. We would not have war at all if everyone could learn how to live with true love, hope and forgiveness.

—Kim Phuc, 6/30/2008

Kim Phuc, nine years old,
running, burning, crying
too hot, too hot
blackened skin peeling
strickened by a single thought—
Too hot made me the ugly girl.

She agonized through 14 months
of grafts and dressing changes
attended by her family
their home destroyed
living day to day
before authorities
put her injuries to use
as propaganda.

Despising cameras
recoiling from strangers
hoping to die
she hid in libraries
took refuge in books
prayed not for a miracle
but how to forgive.

Permitted to travel
studied in Cuba
married a classmate.
On their honeymoon flight
they walked off the plane
requested asylum
while stopped to refuel
on Canadian soil.

Mother of two,
UNESCO ambassador,
Kim Phuc travels the world
telling her story
of love and compassion
to heal the world
as it healed the girl
whose life inspired
a global foundation
assisting child victims of war.

Fifty years later
the girl in the picture
runs toward me
screaming my name.
My eyes meet hers,
the eyes of a child,
a girl, a daughter.

When will we spare
our children from war?
When will our dream
of peace come true?
When will mankind
learn to forgive?

Kim Phuc answers
by posing a question,
the gift of a stone
to place in my shoe—
"If that little girl in the picture
can do it, ask yourself, 'Can't you?'"

Defensive Drivers

Send me forth, dear Lord
among my reckless brothers.
Guide us on our crooked miles
each a hazard to the others.

Multitaskers on the phone
dealing with a crisis,
delivery drivers snatching glances
at their GPS devices.
Single parents late for work
dropping children off at school.
Student drivers at the wheel
making up the rules.
School bus drivers stopping
at their appointed corners,
funeral processions
of limos full of mourners.

Praise defensive drivers
who at God's bidding speed
like grains of sand
through an hour glass
barely far enough apart
to let each other safely pass.

The Long Game

If God created the world
and God is good,
why does evil exist?
The answer, at least
the best I've seen,
is the parable of weeds and wheat
from Matthew's gospel, chapter 13.

If you pull up the weeds
you might uproot the wheat as well.

In the field of living things
whose roots profusely intertwine
could anyone unravel
the good from the malign?

Let them grow together
until the harvest.

Spoken like the God
who causes sun
to rise, the rain to fall
the same for everyone.

Spoken like the God
whose fields are vast,
whose belated justice
leaves followers aghast.

But come the gospel's ending
all that's ample, righteous, blessed
is gathered to the barn.
The weeds go up in flame.

We should have guessed.
Where we see good's defeat
God stakes a higher claim.
Where humans yield to doubt,
the Savior plays a longer game.

Five

The Reunion Float

The Drive-In

In search of sights
our grandkids might not see again
we pulled into a drive-in theater
a relic of the Sixties
entered through a cattle gate
off a throwback road
made obsolete by faster
four-lane interstates.

A screen of white-washed metal sheets
loomed large above a field
not sown for crops but posts
for mounting speakers to the tops.
We eased into an inclined parking spot,
front-end raised,
affording us a better view
while daylight waned
and pre-show business
was attended to—
lining up to use a smelly john,
picking out refreshments
tinted by the glow
of snack bar neon signs,
our faces mirrored by
displays, a chorus line
of giant candy bars and boxes
that seemed to strut behind the glass
while popcorn sputtered,
puffing out a mesmerizing haze
of melted butter.

Well supplied, we settled in,
kids in front, elders in the back
all silenced by a beam of light
that leapt from the projector
in a blaze so bright
it seemed to hustle out the dusk
and usher in the night.

As if revving up a dream
the screen went wild with Looney Tunes
untamed animation
whose raucous fits and throes
put to shame
anything as tame
as a Disney or a Pixar show.

Highjacked by cartoon characters
we became the passengers
in imaginary flight
ready to succumb and go
along with the illusions
of the feature show—
Gremlins—the Mogwai's story
of pets no human could resist
much less foresee the aftermath
of broken rules of care and feeding.

Don't get a Mogwai wet.
Keep them out of solar light,
and never, ever, ever
feed them after midnight.

Of course, a feckless character forgets.
A single moment of neglect
begets a horde of scaly monsters
that terrorize the town.

From the safety of our car,
our grandkids take delight
in gremlin mayhem
gone from bad to worse
from worse to deadly craziness.

In the end, a boy named Billy saves the day.
The gremlins, tricked,
blow themselves to bits,
while Gizmo, the good,
the Mogwai like no other
undoes a skylight curtain
to incinerate his last surviving brother.

From that night on, *Gremlins* is the grandkids favorite show,
a fable told of magic gone too far.
Driving home, they dream up Mogwai of their own
while in the front seat of the car
my wife and I exchange a glance.

Dear Lord, what have we grown-ups done?
What rules did we forget about
the care and feeding of the young?

Judy and Clark

A hummingbird
lured by sugar water
flew into a trap, soft-sided
made of mesh,
a scarlet box
hanging from a line
like a mid-air lobster pot.

A gentle hand transferred the bird
to a drawstring cotton bag
passed to an even gentler hand,
Verne's, the master bander,
who with pressure
of a thumb and middle finger.
restrained the wings
while pliers in his other hand
looped a numbered
band around a tiny leg.
The business done,
Verne placed the bird,
immobile, overcome,
into the hollow of
my grandson's hand.

Clark called her Judy,
as if they'd met before.
Time seemed to stop
until, with another bird to band,
Verne tapped the underside
of Clark's immobile hand.

Wings a-blur
the path of Judy's flight
would trace a skyway of chiffon.
We watched her,
wheeling out of sight
but only Clark could tell
when she was really gone.

Independence Day

I dreamed of glazed, cobblestone streets
in Philadelphia around Independence Hall.
Pedestrians were slipping but not me.
The soles of my shoes had spikes
holding fast, like ideas that matter.
A*ll men are created equal,* for one.
*Endowed with certain inalienable right*s
for another. *Consent of the governed*
make three on the slippery streets of self-governance.

The tall red-haired gentleman beside me
was Thomas Jefferson, struggling to stay on his feet
but too independent to ask for help.
I took his arm and steadied him
to demonstrate that two could form
a more perfect union.
He couldn't bring himself to thank me, though.
He grumped, "In Monticello, it doesn't snow,"
as if to blame the North for icy roads
or lack of slaves to get the plowing done.
As frosty as they come, Mr. Jefferson,
but who could better frame
the hope of liberty America became?

Antiques Roadshow

I am the Newcomb College vase glazed in muted tones
the Confederate belt buckle, emblazoned CSA.
The stained glass lamp . . . could it be?
The markings on my base confirm a Tiffany.
The basket in your hands
was made of Arizona grasses
so tightly crafted even water
scarcely passes through.

I wait in line with you and fellow heirloom holders
admiring one another's curios and treasures.
Here, a clock for calculating longitude
to fix a ship's position.
There, a model train by Lionel, its value doubled
by the box in mint condition.
Here, a Turkish prayer rug, double-knotted
colorized by plant-based dyes
a rug so greatly prized,
so rarely to appear
only two have come to market in more than 20 years.

At our approach, the appraiser's eyes go wide.
She sets me on a spinning pedestal
to elaborate on each detail
while I enjoy the ride.

What other show compares to Antiques Roadshow,
itself an antique as television series go?
The U.S. version on the air
since 1997, half treasure hunt, half street fair
back when people still said, "on the air."

I am the cherished trove
assembled by the love of all things old and rare
inherited, passed along
found in attic, cedar chest or loft
tucked away in places now forgotten.
You put us there to keep from being lost.

In the queue we mingle
in hopes of being chosen for a cameo
appearance on the show.
Well worth the wait to chat with experts
glad to pass on everything they know,
no airs put on or nonchalance
but pleased to meet and talk with you
about your item's provenance.

At last the leading expert speaks,
the climax of an antique's tale.
Have you ever had the piece appraised?
Abashed, you shake your head
while connoisseurs
composed and calm
smile knowingly
before they drop the bomb—

At retail, twenty thousand dollars
if not more, depending on the outcome
of an auction bidding war.

Incredulous,
you shake your head in wild surmise,
blinking as if blinded by a spotlight beam
aimed straight into your eyes.

If I and other heirlooms on display
could speak, what might we say?
How might we toast this lightning bolt
that takes your breath away?

Here's to you, PBS
for season after season
of honoring the past.
From vantage of our comfy chairs
the program goes too fast.

Here's to rare discoveries,
until for heaven's sake
an honored antique kept for years
turns out to be a fake.

Here's to you, the thrift store denizen
whose triumphant grin and eyes
seem to utter quietly
Won't my husband be surprised?

Here's to you, the hero of the story
for having had the courage
to keep possessions others called absurd.
If not for you, they might have hauled me
out and thrown me to the curb.

In the end, here's to artifacts
gone by a thousand times without a second glance
until the Roadshow stopping by
gave me another chance.

All's forgiven now.
For all the times you walked right by a legacy
a heritage that's yours and yours alone
suspected all along and worthy of a show.
The difference being this—
instead of wondering, now you know.

Migratory Elders

We old men are September birds
without an ounce of passion
for anything but feeding
in the midst of molting
when color, territory,
song and breeding
have no charm to calm our frenzy
for seeds and nuts, berries, fruit of any kind,
all the oils, sugars, fats and carbs
summer leaves behind.

We've made it through the molt
re-feathering our shafts and barbs
snug in vests of fat
juiced with hormone overflow.
When daylight wanes
like convicts in a prison break
we break our chains and go.

The Reunion Float

The Class of 1953,
floats down Main Street
like survivors on a raft
in the stream
of our small town's
autumn festival.
Transported on a float,
reunited, on parade
with fellow graduates
enthroned on folding chairs
or benches made of bales of hay
on a flat bed trailer
in tow behind a snorting
John Deere, coughing smoke
with each clutch and shift,
a mile of stop-and-go
down Main Street
from the Amtrak station
to the courthouse square.
Old friends point them out and cheer.
Dogs bark, as if to say in human speech—
Meet us in the park!

The royalty of the festival
ride reunion floats, one for every
fifth and tenth year class.
They seem to age before our eyes
5th, 10th, 15th, 20th,
followed by more ancient classes
pleased to mingle with old loves
or grant reprieve to stubborn grudges.

They hug, shake hands, observe
their peers—how far they've come—
how in each other's eyes
they remain forever young.

Bringing up the rear
are graduates from 1953,
the 70th reunion class,
nobility upon a royal barge
accompanied by high school athletes,
marching bands, town officials,
Boy Scout troops, 4H ribbon winners,
a court of beauty queens
flaunting first-place sashes
showing off their princess waves
swept up in small-town pageantry
that phones and cameras will save.

In an hour or so
the parade becomes a barbecue
at picnic tables, under tents
beside the silent bronzes
of battle monuments.
The living chatter on about
the weather, local businesses
somehow holding on
late August storms that saved the crops
heads bowed for neighbors gone.

The last to disembark
is an 88-year-old.
Steadied by a younger hand
the elder seems to say—
If you're lucky,
you'll be riding on a float
in 70 years.

Yes I looked like you,
full head of hair
standing tall, not even trying.
There were 26 of us back then,
full of hope and promise
now whittled down to six,
outliving spouses, children, neighbors
at rest beneath the stones on cemetery lawns.
We visit, reminisce,
mourn and move along,

Tethered to each other
by a common point in time,
who'd have guessed in '53
we'd go on seven decades more?
Our float affirms a passing generation
sturdier and more connected
than anyone expected.

See us in our open boat.
Listen. Hear us cry—
We made it you and I
on seas of love and grief
heaving on the swells of time
to overtake a disappearing fleet.

About the Author

Kevin Shyne is a lifelong writer, whose career included 12 years as a freelance magazine writer and 23 years as a corporate speechwriter. Writing poetry in his spare time, he took a deeper dive into creative writing after his retirement in 2013.

Kevin and his wife Debi raised their two daughters in the Chicago suburbs, before moving to Princeton, a small town in North Central Illinois.

Kevin is active in the Illinois River Valley poetry community, taking part in poetry readings and critique workshops. In 2023, Kevin and a small group of volunteers organized *Poetic Voices,* showcasing the poetry of seven local poets. Previously the same group of volunteers organized *The Festival of the Written Word,* a one-day celebration of creative writing for students at eight high schools in Bureau County, Illinois.

Kevin writes poetry to discover, record, and reflect on observations that might otherwise be lost in the swirling current of day-to-day living. Kevin is the author of *The Faith of Fragile Things,* a collection of poems published in 2022 by Kelsay Books. His poems have also been published in numerous journals and recognized in poetry competitions sponsored by the Niles (Illinois) Public Library and *The Bureau County Republican* newspaper.

www.ingramcontent.com/pod-product-compliance
Lightning Source LLC
LaVergne TN
LVHW020655100826
845148LV00012B/2508

* 9 7 8 1 6 3 9 8 0 6 2 6 3 *